Unseeable

A short story about the long process of healing
and a shared hope for others enduring
the effects of trauma.

Chapters

Acknowledgements

It would be impossible to name all the amazing souls who have been a part of my healing journey, from authors and speakers to family and friends, many who unknowingly had a profound impact on my life. I pray that my life, this work, and the works to come are an honorable echo of gratitude to all the outstanding individuals who have played a part in my becoming and unbecoming. To mention some is to risk failing to mention others, and so I leave it at this: If you know me, you're a part of this story, unquestionably. If we have yet to meet, I sure hope one day we do.

Dedication

To my Alicen Rose,
without whom I would have given up
the pursuit of being my best.

Introduction

Since you're holding this book in your hands, you may likely find yourself being curious or desperate, or maybe you land somewhere in between. Perhaps you've endured a trauma yourself and are seeking reassurance that there is more to life than the spinning cycles of reactivity. In the best spoiler alert ever, let me inform you that there is more, so much more. It could be that you're watching a loved one navigate the effects of trauma, and you're reading to gain insight into what life is like in their shoes or how you may come alongside them in support. If so, I love that about you. Maybe you have an insatiable desire to hear the stories of others, the struggles that stifled them and the courage they've found to conquer. Welcome, friend. I too am a lover of stories. Truth be told, I have found myself in each of these places, and many more, so no matter the reason, I'm glad you're here.

I want to begin by disclosing that in no way am I an expert on trauma, unless you give credit hours for a lifetime of accumulated experience. Even then, my own poor choices made out of immaturity or a lack of healing could be grounds for disqualification of expert status. This seems like a great time for a disclaimer: I am the kind of person to call things out - quite directly. That applies to myself and others. I don't sugar coat anything, though I have been working on softening my approach. Pretending like I was not immature or did not make unhealthy choices out of a lack of healing would have thwarted my progress, both in the past and moving forward. I refuse. I am a lifelong learner; a seeker of wisdom and growth. This to me is the essence of the maturing process. Undoubtedly, we all have experienced stagnation with this a time or ten, whether that be with ourselves or with another.

I have an unquenchable curiosity for life, fascinated by the experiences we endure and what we enjoy. I love learning the many varied perspectives we each bring to our shared human experience. It is my deepest hope and strongest desire that this book fills you with hope for healing, particularly if others have attempted to get you to believe it is not possible or you've fallen prey to the casualty of apathy yourself. If you've caught yourself wondering if this is as good as it gets, then the answer is yes. It is. Unless you decide to change it. The stories and experiences you'll read about are decades in the making. One day, one month, one year after another, I was blissfully discontent with life and decided to change mine. The process has felt unbearable at times, though more than anything, I want to assure you that the outcomes have been worth every effort.

My journey has been just as much about unlearning and unbecoming as anything else. I spent more time than I care to admit feverishly collecting opinions of others and negotiating my worth, before finally coming to a place of love and acceptance. I think, feel, and choose in very unique ways, and so do you. Despite, and perhaps more accurately because of our differences, we are a wonderful tapestry of human experience and human design; each of us a beautiful masterpiece, individually representing an aspect of the Limitless Love that intended us into existence. Coming to a place of approving of myself and giving myself the freedom to be fully me has been a tumultuous ride, and I am thrilled to share a part of that with you.

We get this one wild life. We get one chance to live this crazy adventure to the fullest. Gratefully, if we have participated in less than stellar ways, we have unlimited chances to start over - each moment, each day - we can begin again the important work of becoming our best selves. Truly, within our one chance at this grand expedition of life, we have limitless chances to learn, grow, and transform. Trauma can and does absolutely shape us. Despite the undeniable realities of what we have faced, the future can be even greater than anything we would have dared to dream in our darkest moments. As you read on, I hope you dare to dream again.

I'll share a glimpse to where this exhilarating mission has gotten me at this point, as well as a look back at the moment that forever changed everything. In the face of such realities, many of us have further moments, grappling for traction at making sense of life after intense loss. You'll hear some of those stories as well, before circling back around to the breakthroughs and tools that helped me build the life I love. Perhaps through it all, you'll have a hope restored, a joy rekindled, or an insight ignited. And maybe, just maybe, more meaning will be brought from the madness of this life I've lived.

Now

I'm beginning in what may seem an unusual way. Learning about my life now might feel unnecessarily tedious, but I promise there's a method and a message. Before diving into the drudgery of trauma, I want to fill you with the perhaps mundane insights into what life can be like after enduring the unseeable. Are other people's lives more exciting, successful, or interesting? Probably. But here you are reading this book, so I'll give it my best shot, encapsulating the victories accumulated along the way to creating a life I love. Hopefully, by the end of the last sentence in the last chapter, you'll share in the excitement I have in this beautifully, remarkably ordinary life, marked by tragedy as I barely began my adulthood. More importantly, if you have any area of struggle in your own life, I hope that through reading this, you feel encouraged to live more hopefully, pursuing your own healing and trusting that there is beauty available to us all on the other side of the pain. I hope that you live your life unapologetically authentic and fully present. This story isn't the one I ever wanted to tell. Little girls, even those who read all the books and one day dream of writing them never, I assure you, never dream of having a story like this to tell. Nevertheless, I do. I am. And for all of the harshness within it, it is nevertheless beautiful.

As I write this, I am sitting at my dining room table. The wind is rustling through the trees as the falling leaves remind me of the beauty in letting go. In my home and around my acreage are an unlimited number of reminders that life as a single mom is challenging, and many things go undone. The laundry basket is overflowing because, in this house, it takes a few hours to wash and dry laundry but approximately seven to ten business days for it to be put away. There are dishes on the kitchen countertop, a dishwasher that needs to be unloaded, and gorgeous wooden floors forever in need of being swept thanks to two dogs constantly running in and out, cats that sneak in, and a host of kids stopping by to say hi. The landscaping needs what I can presume to be thousands of dollars and hundreds of hours' worth of work, neither of which are readily available at this time. The sliding glass door to my deck is open, masking some of the handprints and paw prints, as I enjoy the unusual warmth flirting with fall season, a welcome experience for early November.

Earlier today, I soaked up sunshine on the other side of that sliding door, thinking of you. Knowing I would be sitting down moments later, what would I want to share with you? How would I outline and articulate the varied experiences amassed through these past twenty three years, two months, eighteen days, and thirty three minutes? The oddly specific time will make more sense in the next chapter. Defining moments of our lives often become a landmark, the anniversaries of which become an invitation to grieve yet again what once was and an incentive to celebrate what has become. This writing is for me just that - a revelry of overcoming what I once thought impossible to endure. The lightness of jubilee is greater than any depth of grief I've ever experienced. Perhaps that is the most important highlight I hope you capture - the blissfulness of healing happens when we learn to love and feel at home in the lightness of being, letting it replace the heavy familiarity of darkness and the drudgery of relinquishing ourselves to the past. We don't exist there any longer. While the past indelibly shapes us, our status as prisoners to it expires when we choose to make meaning from the mess and move forward.

By all rights and reasons, I live a "normal" life, whatever that means. I am in the final stretch of raising my youngest child, a smart and funny young lady who has big goals to finish high school as Valedictorian. My two grown children have successfully flown the nest, each of whom brings me a wild sense of pride. My son is currently in an extensive advanced training program for serving our country, and the challenges of being away from him present a whole different type of struggle. My oldest daughter is breaking generational chains and blazing her own path in life in ways that inspire me and others, most likely far more than she could imagine. For the past five years I have also been enthralled in the bliss of grandparenting. For all the joys of raising her mother, my granddaughter is my reward for surviving the challenges. Though I have had my fair share of struggles in mom life, I love this gig. It is so fun. They are all truly amazing humans, all superbly uniquely adding to the richness and vibrancy of my life, and that of countless others as they expand their reach in their own ways. It is a great honor to be their mother and I most likely don't do an adequate job of telling them so. Becoming a mom at such a young age, only seventeen, shaped my entire identity. It was not until about a decade ago, when I decided to figure out who I really was, that I alleviated some of the stress and pressure I unconsciously put on myself and my children. I am still making amends and working to heal aspects of the damage done through my years of being an overbearing and micromanaging mother.

If we bumped into one another in a public place, you may not think there's really anything extraordinary about me. If it weren't for my own personal beliefs that we are all created with extraordinary greatness and unique purpose, I would absolutely agree with you. I would hope that upon our meeting and getting to know me a bit, you would feel empowered and encouraged in some way, though since I am utterly human, that may depend on circumstances. While entirely imperfect, I do my best to leave people, places, and things better than I found them, though I would be remiss if I didn't admit that I have appropriately been accused of being "a Karen" more than once, a term not so affectionately given to those women who have a proclivity to be bossy or demanding. Thankfully, my healing has brought a calm to that storm as well. Embracing softness and gentleness on the back side of enduring trauma can feel so incredibly uneasy at first. I have learned to bring the energy I want to experience in life, rather than letting myself be caught up in the environment, pushed and pulled about like a paper bag in the wind, and rather than feverishly attempting to control circumstances for a false sense of stability. That was a long, exhausting learning curve with limitless stories.

I live a modest life, for now, but get me talking about my goals and dreams for the future, and you'll see a whole other side of me. I have great, big dreams and goals to pursue and thanks to my experiences holding the flashlight and fetching tools for my dad growing up, I have the resilience to do so. Just kidding. Kind of. (I mean… if you know, you know.) Even with my grand plans for the future, trust that I'll be a collector of experience, rather than things. I am an adventurer at heart with grand desires to see and experience the world, the cultures and curiosities that make life exciting. I'm also a simple woman, other than my decorated skin, adorned with ink to remind me of monumental moments of life. My clothing is primarily chosen for comfort, and rarely do I apply anything more than mascara or lip gloss, and even those are limited. You won't find me with fancy nails or adorned with extravagant bling. Material items are of little importance to me, though there's no shame at all in fancying the finer things in life. My tendency is just towards any kind of exploration more than acquisition. Not uncommonly you'll catch me enjoying what may even be laughable to others, its value found only in the memories I've attached to the symbolism of the object itself. All of that really is unimportant information shared merely to illustrate the point that after enduring what you're about to read, life truly can rebalance to a beautiful normalcy; a sacred space of peacefulness can exist where chaos once consumed.

In addition to offering you a little window into my life, my greatest hope is that despite all its imperfections, ongoing challenges, and stressors, what you will glean is the gift of hope that lies in the journey of healing. And can I let you in on a little secret? I believe the journey is the destination. Far too often, they are presented as mutually exclusive, and I think we've been sold a false bill of goods. A false focus on then and there robs us of the beauty of now. The life I am living today would feel surreal, considering all the circumstances, if I hadn't been the one living out my days with a tenacity to make it so. More often than not, my days are filled with purpose, joy, and laughter. My home is a peaceful place, filled with love. It is often a revolving door to many extra kids, some who come over to talk after a breakup, or just because they need a hug. I have become the safe space I needed, and I have opened that sense of safety to others who need it as well. These gifts and experiences gathered along the path to wholeness are priceless treasures.

There are still times, even after several years in business, that I sit back in awe and wonder. I get to do this; I get to be me. Day after day, week after week, I get to meet with clients to support them on their healing journey in mind, body, and spirit. Meeting others in whatever stage of life and struggle they find themselves in is an honor. Holding space for and empowering others is a passionate purpose I am thrilled to pursue. Whether I am meeting my clients virtually or in person, in my practice, I am trusted to be an advisor and encourager; to help my clients discover the root causes of imbalance and promote their wellness with a variety of natural resources. It is a sacred privilege I do not take for granted. Pursuing my education and building a successful practice for almost a decade now has been an immeasurable blessing. The old saying goes that if you do what you love, you'll never work a day in your life. It is true. It doesn't feel much like work when it is pursued with purpose. And now, I get to do *this*. I get to share my story of hope and healing in a way that has the chance to reach more hearts and minds. Reading and writing have been healthy outlets of peaceful release since I was a young girl.

Not only do I have a thriving practice as a certified traditional Doctor of Naturopathy, life coach, and energy practitioner, I am also blessed with an abundance of relationships with family and friends, near and far. They add tremendous value to my life, and I seek to reciprocate that by blessing their lives as well. Today, I am the best mom I have ever been. Today, I am the best grandma I have ever been. Today,

I am the best holistic health practitioner I have ever been. Today, I am the best friend, sister, daughter, and self I have ever been. In these precious connections, we live, love, and laugh together. We cry together and call one another out compassionately when we miss the mark and fail to uphold our own standards of excellence. We engage in life together, and each of us are enriched by our own and one another's efforts. None of that is said to be pretentious. It is shared with abundant thankfulness for the ways that others have welcomed me into their lives as well. It is shared in humble gratitude, with the utmost reverence for the Divine Love that pursued me relentlessly, refining me and growing me to be my best. In doing so, I have been able to contribute more consciously to my own life and the lives of others. I have walked through valleys of shame, guilt, betrayal, trauma, unforgiveness, and more. Never once have I been ultimately rejected or abandoned, though I have felt the sting of both. Always was I given chances to learn and grow, even if they escaped my awareness momentarily.

Throughout my writings, you'll hear references to my faith. It is unapologetically a cornerstone of my life and a firm foundation upon which my healing rests. There is an unshakable knowing within my soul that there is a Higher Power to which and through which we are all inextricably interconnected. I may reference many labels or names associated with this Magnificent Maker that, I believe, invoked each one of us with purpose, intention, and special giftedness. I love that I can wholeheartedly celebrate each person as a unique reflection of the vast Creative Energy by which we were designed. That may very well be the reason we are here on this rock, spinning in an expansive universe, as beautiful souls having a very, very human experience - to learn to love and appreciate ourselves and one another. As I dive deeper in the chapters to come about some of my most pivotal experiences, you'll see how my faith anchored me, times when I went adrift, and how I fought to free myself from the projections of fallacies or confines of religious constructs to move into treasured authenticity.

Spirituality is a nuanced subject, and I am incredibly tender to the wounding that can come from God's people. Been there. Done that. Got the shirt, and do not care to ever again buy a ticket to that theme park. Please don't misunderstand me to be a cynical saint. I am a grateful believer. I treasure my weekly opportunities to fellowship, share in collective worship, and listen to gifted teachers. I just do so now from a place of greater spiritual freedom and groundedness, completely content with letting others have their beliefs and having my own. Disagreement does not equal rejection. If you are struggling with your faith, let me assure you dear one, that is totally reasonable. I've got that shirt too. As you'll read later on, and even more so in books to come, separating God from other believers and especially from restrictive theologies has been one of the greatest breakthroughs in my healing process. Each of us has our own unique journey through life in mind, body, and spirit. We get the opportunity to enjoy shared moments and stories together.

As I close out this reflection of the beauty of now, it is not lost on me that far too frequently when the heaviness of trauma is suffocating, it feels nearly impossible to believe in the possibilities of healing and a Benevolent Divinity that could have permitted such pain to permeate the human existence. It takes courage to persevere, to seek more in life, so if no one else has done so, let me say congratulations, audacious one. Whether it is in stories that we read, podcasts we listen to, our own ramblings through writings, or even in the blissful solitude of seeking stillness to rest in, learning more about ourselves and others is a brave thing. Taking spectacular care of myself has become a triumphant part of my healing journey. The hardest part was believing I was worth it, adopting to my identity a sense of ownership for building a life I love, rather than abdicating myself to an obligation to get through. No matter where on the vast spectrum you find yourself, please know that you are seen, heard, and treasured. There is a Heavenly Light that flows in a beautiful invisible currency through each of us. We are all inextricably interconnected.

You are here for a purpose. You were created with greatness. Who you are makes a difference. Now matters. If it is not everything you desire for it to be, you have the divine right and responsibility to welcome the new. New is possible, even inevitable if you are willing to put in the effort. You are worth wellness, beloved.

Then

The noise of unidentifiable objects clashing against the basement wall rumbled up the stairs. I remember wondering what in the world he could possibly be throwing around down there that was making such a ruckus. The yelling echoed, as I busied myself in my most precious, though often overwhelming, role. On August 20th, 2000 while chaos around consumed, my otherwise fiercely independent toddler was providing a welcome distraction of demands. Requesting one thing after another to refuel her belly after a not long enough nap. I walked through the kitchen, void of cabinet doors from previous outbursts of her father's drunken anger, while his newest wave of rage rang up the stairs and down the hall. It was a day mostly like any other day, except today he hadn't been drinking. This made the hostility that much more unsettling, that much more worthy of avoidance. He was outrageously against the boundary I had set - he needed to leave until he could get help for his anger and drinking problems. He needed help. We needed help. I just couldn't do it anymore.

He was a wonderful man, full of love and adoration, a hard working provider, and fun-loving, unless he had been drinking. He was hilarious and affectionate. He would come home from work all smelly and sweaty, chasing me around the house before hopping in the shower. He rarely called me by my name, instead giving me a few tender nicknames. He loved our little girl so much. He was a doting daddy, very protective of our tiny little princess. Given only a three percent chance to live, he took her little life very seriously, not permitting anyone to give her too many sweets or treats. He catered to her pickiness, making sure her food was just the right temperature or that she always had access to her favorite toys. He wanted her to be healthy and strong, and everyone knew better than to challenge him on anything to do with his little diva. One weekend a month, he would go serve our country and talked often of doing more training and even taking deployments. On the good days, I laughed inside at the possibilities of that, considering how hard it seemed to be for him to be away for just a weekend. On the bad days, I wished he would go.

The stressors of our attempt at doing life the right way as two very young parents, only nineteen and twenty-one at the time of his death, led him to drink. A lot. We had already been attempting our efforts for over two years, and the issues just kept escalating. I believed every sober word in the mornings that followed the nights we both would rather have forgotten. I genuinely do not believe he wanted to be acting in such horrific ways. Oftentimes, he would cry for hours as he examined new evidence of yet another night he promised would never happen again. I wholeheartedly believe he had deeply rooted problems far beyond his own awareness that perpetuated our dysfunctional existence. The occasional fat lip if my reflexes weren't on point, the holes in the walls, and the kicked out or punched out kitchen cabinet doors were a chronically visible reminder that we were broken. The fact that I stayed and tolerated such an environment bore witness to my own remarkably persistent issues with codependency, lack of boundaries, and nearly non-existent standards. They were also proof of my unyielding optimism and insistence on ignoring reality in favor of a hopeless romantic outcome.

The weeks leading up to that fateful day were filled with tears, fights, empty promises, and endless demonstrations that the struggles we were facing exceeded what we were equipped to handle. I recall feeling like I was stuck in a horrible dramatization of the movie *Groundhog Day*. One day of insanity after another, and though we both seemed aware of the cycles, we were either unwilling or unable to break the chains. The weeks to come would be far more stressful than I had anticipated as I was planning for our wedding on September 9, 2000. I could sell myself on the story of him going to treatment or outgrowing the pattern of drinking that had become so prolific. I knew we both had so much growing and maturing to do. What I could not get any part of myself to condone was the immeasurable betrayal of his recent infidelity, regardless of whether it had been brought on by yet another night of overindulgence, particularly when he displayed a powerlessness to prevail in quitting.

I had become numb to the word sorry and apathetic to his plea for more chances. The chill of indifference packs a punch, too, even if it doesn't leave a mark. I have no doubt that my cold disposition and detachment caused damage of its own to the environment of our home, the reality of which became a platform for a tremendous amount of healing work through the years as I grieved, released guilt, grew, and gained the grace to forgive myself fully. At the time, I would have had a hard time realizing the weight of my own attitudes and actions. His own hurtful, harmful conduct did not excuse the brutality of my dispassionate posture towards him. Realizing that we, at any given moment, are doing the best we can and that we can do better is a richly rewarding paradox to embrace.

Now that you have some background to the environment of our home at the time, I want to bring you back with me to the day that forever changed my life. Our daughter, just two months shy of her second birthday, was startled awake from her nap by our failed endeavors to problem solve. Again. I recall feeling absolutely exasperated. I was confronted with my failures as a mom to protect my child from the damaging effects of a fragmented family. We were so broken. I just wanted to cuddle her, console her, read her a book, and pretend life would be fine. She wanted snacks and juice, so I took her to the kitchen and proceeded to gather her goodies. I looked at her sweet face and marveled at how in the world I got so lucky, and then wondered how I could make her little world right when my own was such a mess. Her smile and sweet little voice, innocently asking for yogurt and animal crackers despite all the havoc around us penetrated my heart, and I whispered a silent prayer for change. Something had to change. It would, and he would go. It would just happen in ways I never expected.

In my exhaustion, I was all but entirely disengaged. He wanted a hug, a kiss, some kind of reassurance that we would be ok somehow. He seemed to be unraveling in the realization that the brokenness was now unavoidable. I wanted to be left alone. I was hurt, confused, and overwhelmed with the new level of hell that had overtaken our home. In finally standing my ground, I urged him downstairs to pack a bag. Where he went was irrelevant - I only wanted him gone. We could talk later but I needed time to gather my thoughts and get back to feeling anything beyond the then current complacency. Little did I know, I would be numb for a long while. His appeals felt endless, matched only by my ability to ignore them. He finally relented, noisily. I remember wondering how a man had so many questions about his own belongings, as he shouted out seekings of where this or that was, and ongoing demands for me to get downstairs. It only increased my frustrations, exposing how much I had enabled an unreasonable imbalance of responsibility.

The moments that followed are eternally embedded in my memory. On August 20, 2000 at 2:12 p.m., I was at the kitchen sink, wetting a washcloth to clean up my baby girl's messiness. The loud clap of the shotgun startled me; the smell of gunpowder and death mingled in the air, assaulting my senses. None of it was anything I had ever experienced before, and yet somehow my mind was able to identify the uncomfortable aromas and ear-piercing sound. As my mind raced to process my new unavoidable reality, I felt frozen. My heart was racing, and yet the blood seemed to stop flowing through my body entirely. I felt cold. I couldn't breathe. I couldn't see straight. My mind was spinning. I stood there with the water running, unable to move. I looked over at the kitchen table where my daughter was turned backwards on her chair, her tiny fingers gripping the rounded back so tightly that her knuckles were as white as the chair. Her face was smeared with blueberry yogurt, announcing her independence in eating it all by herself. Her big brown eyes stared into mine with thousands of questions, and I had no answers. She seemed to instinctively know that something was terribly, disastrously wrong. She didn't move. I didn't move. We just were; lost together, in a split second that lasted an eternity.

When I could finally move, I didn't want to. I didn't want to know what I knew that I knew. The sound of silence is eerie in moments like that. For as much as I wanted the yelling to stop and the throwings to cease, I would have traded anything in that moment for those sounds to return. I couldn't call his name. I couldn't utter a sound. I set the washcloth on the table and welcomed her independence to clean herself up, hoping she wouldn't follow me. Thankfully she didn't. As I cautiously walked down the stairs, streams of sunlight from the window danced with the shotgun smoke that now infused the air. I remember trembling uncontrollably. Nothing could have prepared me for what I found when I entered through the basement door. I screamed a thousand screams in a split second, though I'm not sure if I actually uttered a sound. Regardless of any challenges encountered, seeing the lifeless body of the man I loved, the father of my child, was a reality I could not process. Seeing the unseeable. It changes you. Forever.

I remember calling 911, annoyed by the questions of the dispatcher. As much as I myself operate out of insatiable curiosity, that was not the time for questions. Somehow they failed to understand the dire circumstances. No, he could not be breathing without a brain. I wondered if I was failing to convey the reality I didn't want to be facing somehow, or if they were just thoroughly doing their job. Either way, in my reaction to this trauma, I didn't have the patience for it. I just wanted someone, anyone, to show up and make it all go away. I knew it was not going away. It was real, even if it didn't feel real. I remember calling my parents and finally feeling a sense of soothing as I heard their voices. I remember sitting on the driveway, leaned up against our old red Pontiac, waiting for both to arrive. I remember the police officer who ran out of the house and vomited in my flower bed. I couldn't cry. I just stared off into the distance in disbelief. As my parents drove us away from where we once called home, I called my boss to let her know I wouldn't be at work Monday morning, and her asking if he was going to be ok, clearly exposing her inability to process the horror I disclosed. I remember simply reiterating, "No. He's dead."

The room at the police station was cold, or maybe I was just still cold. I was shaking. I couldn't stop shaking, no matter how hard I tried. The investigators did their best to make the stale environment more welcoming, asking if they could get me anything and explaining the process that was unfolding before me. I don't know that I could really comprehend anything at that time. I was given an opportunity to have an attorney present and remember feeling confused. Why would I need one? I was required to give a recorded statement and have my hands dusted for gunshot residue to rule out any foul play. I understood everything going on to the best of my limited ability, which was minimal since I didn't understand anything about my life at that time. How could someone, anyone, be involved in such acts? Murder had never been more of a mystery than in that moment. Somehow, it was all simultaneously a blur and each moment was also frozen in time, lived in slow motion. After giving my recorded statement, the recording device was turned off. I can still hear the way it sounded, as the halt resounded through the silence that remained. I remember the investigator looking at me and telling me I was one of the lucky ones, knowing not all women survive such domestic violence situations, particularly since many who are suicidal also become homicidal. "With all due respect, sir, I don't feel very lucky."

Even then, in that phase of my life where my faith was faint, there was a Supreme Power that held me together. There was a silent stillness that carried me down those stairs and back up. There was a voice that spoke in and through me to make the calls and answer the seemingly endless questions. There was a peace that surpassed all understanding even then. It would have all been utterly impossible for me to endure otherwise. The Powerful Presence didn't require my acknowledgment to be. It just was and is. Having been raised with faith, I knew and believed that God was with me, and I am grateful for that. I did not blame God for my fiancé's choices. As a stubborn, rebellious woman, I have always been quite thankful for free will. Being raised with a strong undercurrent of personal responsibility reaffirmed that each of us is accountable for our own actions. I believe the early shaping of those mindsets allowed me a great deal of openness in continuing my faith in the face of such fearful times. That being said, I certainly did not lean on my faith to get me through. In hindsight, I can see that it unquestionably delayed many aspects of my overcoming. These reflections looking back fill me with thankfulness that the Universe is patiently constant.

Impact

The months that followed his suicide were like being on a roller coaster I never bought a ticket for and there was no chicken exit. Who am I kidding - even if there were, between my unending quest for adventure and my unnerving pride at the time, I wouldn't have taken it. I assure you a grin and bear it temperament is not an excitingly adventurous way to treat such dreadfulness. Pride had taken root when I had my daughter at seventeen, determined not to be a cliche teen mom. Though there's awareness and gratitude for my determination to do hard things, I added challenge upon unnecessary challenge by letting fear of failure keep me tethered to self-sufficiency. Allowing myself to acknowledge I needed help let alone ask for it? Highly unusual. Pride proceeded to take over trauma. Admittedly, my self-awareness was dim, but there was an unavoidable recognition that I was not ok, which was systemically stifled. In case you're wondering - that's not suitable for healing. Pride prolonged my misery, though I was completely blind to it at the time. In addition, I had a deep-rooted aversion to feeling like a burden to anyone. I had a mindset at the time that no one else needed to be inconvenienced by my circumstances. The last thing I wanted was pity, despite feeling quite pitiful.

Where the shock had previously created a dam, I quickly found myself able to cry again, and wondered if I would ever be able to stop. Nothing needed to trigger the tears. They flowed like a river, as did a newfound stream of inconsistency. I fluctuated between sleeping excessively and insomnia; eating endlessly and unable to eat; shrouded in silence and non-stop talking. The extremes became my comfort zone, and it was a place I would unknowingly set up camp for years to come. It was anything but comfortable. Even so, the familiarity of swinging from one extreme to another simply gave me a sense of certainty. It was a predictable pattern. I was utterly unraveling in the effects of trauma. I had figured out how to operate in crisis, my nervous system somehow feeling regulated in the dysregulation. There was absolutely no sense of balance, centeredness, or peace. I remember feeling as though I was on the edge of a complete breakdown at all times, pressuring myself to hold it together. I couldn't, I wouldn't let myself fall apart. What I didn't know at the time is that many times, a breakdown leads to a breakthrough. Had I known then what I know now, I might have gotten on with it sooner.

After taking only four days off work to attend to the funeral preparations and avoid the grief that I had no clue how to process, I threw myself back into functioning as best as I could. I suppose part of it was a desire to get back to any kind of normalcy, and the other part was likely just a spectacularly simplistic avoidance technique, readily accepted and even praised in its misunderstandings. Work was a place where I knew how to do what I needed to do, whereas the rest of my life had become a new mystery; a suspenseful drama in a role for which I never auditioned but was permanently cast. There was no understudy for life. I couldn't call in sick or tired, though I was often sick and tired of being sick and tired. The tasks of my job were a welcome reprieve, though I undoubtedly made several mistakes. Trauma had a way of creating clouds of confusion, and an unending onslaught of flashbacks divided my attention with disruptive distractions. My co-workers' well-meaning looks of concern and questions of how I was doing were most likely met with denial. How was I supposed to answer that question, anyway? How is someone supposed to be doing in such circumstances?

I couldn't go back into the home we had shared, the place where he had taken his last desperate breath. It felt haunted and heavy and intensified the effects of my ill-equipped ability to move forward. I didn't even like having to take any of the familiar furnishings with me. In all honesty, I would have preferred to set it all aflame and start over. Not a suitable option, or legal, led friends and family to help pack up the remnants of our life. After staying with my parents for about a month, I found a small rental house for my daughter and I. I continued working, paying bills, and doing all the things to keep us alive, but in reality - we were just not dying. That's not the same thing as living, though it was the best I had to offer. At the risk of being misunderstood, we did the things. We took walks, went to the park, built snowmen, decorated for holidays, and played games. We went shopping, read books, cooked, danced in the kitchen, and watched TV. It's just that I wasn't fully present. I missed so much by going through the motions. I knew the things to do, and did them, each time hoping I might feel something again. Even when I would, it was so fleeting.

A few weeks after his death, I had an epic "Karen" moment. The death certificate arrived in the mail, a necessary document to file for social security benefits for my daughter, as well as finalizing paperwork for many other avenues of moving forward. I recall the wave of absolute rage that ignited in me the instant my eyes scanned each box. Immediate cause of death: Perforating shotgun wound to the head. I was outraged at the unnecessary adjective. I made several unneeded phone calls, demanding answers as to who chose that language. I was filled with a mix of emotions. Anger because I couldn't think of anyone who needed to know it was perforating. I couldn't see how that was a necessary or beneficial description. I thought of others who would also have to read this horror. I feared they would imagine what I could not unsee. Ultimately, I realized it was one of those small circumstances that becomes an outlet for release, not uncommon after suffering a trauma. The small things quite easily become big.

There are many parts of my story in the weeks, months, and years that followed that I am not proud of. I engaged in and allowed things that did not serve my greatest good. That all undeniably impacted my daughter as well, despite her being young and despite my best efforts to shield her from everything I was unraveling in. Some of it I will dive into a little deeper in the chapters to come, though much of it overlaps with other stories for other books at other times. I'll summarize to say that making or entertaining relational decisions without pursuing healing provided more learning experiences, read also as more opportunities to heal from my own harmful choices. There are ways of coping that temporarily relieve the pain, but amplify the impacts of shame afterwards. Zero stars. Not recommended. There is a grief to endure as the effects of trauma are examined in their fullness, and a grace that is granted in compassionate healing. Avoiding the grief did not make it go away. It made it go deeper within. It prolonged my pain, as well as my liberation from it.

My evenings would be filled with cooking and cleaning, books and bath time - all the busyness of single mom life. There was no back up. It was just me and her. I lived for her; such an unreasonable pressure to put on such a tiny life. She was clueless to just how much I counted on her. As the phases of my younger two children and granddaughter's lives have come to those toddler years, I have grieved all over again, realizing the time that was lost with my precious oldest; the time that was stolen by the sacrifice of being a survivor of suicide. Some sacrifices are chosen, and others are unfairly enforced. Suicide unquestionably falls in the latter category. There were memories made and minimally kept in those months and years that followed, blocked by the brain's inability to function optimally without pursuing the healing I didn't know was available on the backside of trauma. Thankfully, I have pictures that captured the reality that we lived and loved. I desired to give my daughter the most normal childhood I could, and I did, despite not being fully present in it.

Every night after tucking her into bed, I would distract myself with reading, movies, chores - anything I could come up with to divert my mind from the inevitable. I remember one night after an exceptionally hard day, feeling like I had no reserves left to fight the night terrors, I washed every dish in my cabinet. I far too frequently pushed myself to the brink of dangerously extreme exhaustion in hopes that sleep would fall upon me before the horrors of my memory had the chance to creep in. I would lie awake in bed every night, terrified to go to sleep. For months, I feared that I would see the unseeable every time I closed my eyes, because I did. When I did finally fall asleep, more often than not, I would be startled awake in the middle of the night, unable to breathe, my heart racing so fast and pounding so hard I felt certain I would die. My mind was unrelenting and I was unable to escape the hellish nightmares and flashbacks. I would scream into my pillow and cry myself back to sleep, only to get up and do it all again the next day. It was a vicious cycle and I had no idea how to break it. I pushed through with the utmost effort I could assemble from the brokenness.

Those experiences tested my faith significantly. I prayed for God to take it all away, and yet it persisted. I begged and bartered, as if speaking to some kind of supernatural salesman or that my words were coins being inserted into some kind of colossal vending machine to get my desired outcome that was constantly out of stock. Despite the unresolved requests, my confidence in my Creator was consistent. What I have come to personally believe is that I was given those most difficult seasons to speak truth to other sufferers. Healing is possible. It is not mine to make sense of. That wouldn't be faith. I was and still am invited into a peaceful trust that all things work together for my good and the glory of the Divine. In this, I have an unshakable confidence.

In an abundance of gratitude, my family came around me and helped in ways I did not know to ask for. Somewhere deep inside, I had enough sense to avoid isolating myself entirely. I recall many conversations with my dad, a Vietnam veteran, on the bench by the backyard pond at my parents' house. He knew trauma, and he knew his daughter. He didn't have to ask if I was ok. He knew there was no way I could be. Sometimes he just sat there in silence with me, smoking his Camel cigarettes, a habit he has since thankfully relinquished. Other times he asked questions or offered advice. Mom would cook comforting meals and call to check in regularly. I always wondered if she knew I was lying when I said I was fine. She would always make sure I was invited to my brother's football games. My sister and I would get together and talk while my nephew and daughter, just three months apart in age, would play. I also had wonderful friendships with my boss and another co-worker. We would get together to share meals, let the kids play, and have at home beauty shop nights. Those people trusted me with wax and hair dye, though I am not sure why, outside of hilarity's sake. They were all so supportive and caring, and made the unbearable more manageable.

While I did my best to show up, I was only partially there. No one really knew what was going on deep inside. I didn't even understand what was going on, so I couldn't imagine attempting to explain it to anyone else. I could have been nominated for an Oscar for my performance, as if life was moving along good enough. Just as much as I had done my best to hide the pain of the abuse and drinking cycles that accumulated in our life before his death, I gave valiant effort towards masking the traumatized effects afterwards. The week before the first anniversary of his death, I was desperate for reprieve. I finally sought medical intervention. The doctor commended me for my efforts, shocked that I had waited so long. He urged me to seek counseling and gave me a gift that charged my rebellious spirit. He prescribed medications to alleviate some of the experienced extremes and told me it was unreasonable to think I could ever function like a normal person again without it. He said, "Some things are just unseeable." I had never really heard that word. Unseeable. Strange to call that all a gift, I know. As you'll read later on, it was exactly what I needed in more ways than one. For all of its unwanted side effects, the medication granted me a recess of the intensity of the overwhelm that had become my life.

One aspect of the impact of his death caught me totally by surprise. The fallout with his family was extensive and utterly soul crushing. We had always been quite disconnected with his mother, for reasons I would not understand until several years later. We had, however, spent so much time with his father, step-mother and their kids. They were truly like another family to me, and I felt so betrayed by the walls that went up between us. At the time I had no real understanding of extreme grief, and how it can cause people to respond and react towards others in shameful ways. There was blame and questions that were impossible to answer, followed by years of missed opportunities for my daughter to continue to experience connection with all that was left of her father. I was so angry at them. My own responses to their hurtful words were harsh. It was hurt upon hurt, as all too often happens in times where loved ones are lost. It is challenging looking back on these realities, particularly when some of them are now gone. Reconciliation comes, and my hope is that if you are in a season of fallout with others, the mention of this will bring hope for healing in those relationships.

Ultimately, the impact of trauma is more extensive than we could ever imagine. What happens in an instant can take days, months, years, and decades in efforts to rebalance. The aftermath can be extensive. Even so, this truth remains and cannot be overstated - healing is possible.

Aftermath

It has taken years for me to be able to look back upon this season of my life without feeling completely overtaken in shame. For so long I was filled with regret for the years where I made compromising choices. That shame unconsciously kept me tethered to cycles of guilt-ridden concessions and compromises to living in the fullness of my value. Even now, self-reproach bubbles up to the surface like hot lava, threatening to set these pages aflame. Nevertheless, it is an important part of the story to tell. My hope is that in sharing with you the insights of options chosen that I wouldn't choose again, you can, as I did, learn to forgive yourself and integrate the fullness of your own story with grace and compassion. It can be true that we are doing the best we can on any given day, considering the space we are in mentally, emotionally, physically, and spiritually and knowing that we can do better.

Each day we can truly give the best of what we have to give, but every day our best can be different.

I think it is also important to note that through all of the cycles you're about to read, I maintained employment, paid all my bills, and most likely appeared to be doing really well, perhaps even thriving. I even bought a house as a single mom. Throughout my adult life, outside of a mortgage payment or small loans that were paid off long before their due dates, I have maintained a debt free lifestyle. Not carrying the stress of a chronic car note and hefty credit card payments allowed me to live in greater peace and freedom. I did not always have much excess, but I always had enough. I was diligent in being a good steward of my resources, living within my means, and planning wisely. The traumatic loss of her father helped me to grasp the importance of being prepared. I was so proud to be able to provide a sense of stability for my daughter in tangible ways, painfully aware of how frequently I failed her in the intangible.

My desire to live a normal life was ever increasing, at rates that my inner reality could not match. I would smile and laugh, put on a brave face, and never ever let anyone know just how deeply I was suffering inside. I would talk about my struggles briefly, and dismissively at that. Using humor to deflect or minimize pain has been a long standing pattern. Mocking the disastrous effects of tragedy somehow made reality more palatable for others, and I was generally sick of it all anyway. It was not uncommon that I would realize the cavalier nature with which I addressed life when I caught a glimpse of that deer in the headlights look in others' eyes as I nonchalantly discussed his death and the resulting aftermath. By avoiding the depth of my pain, I merely prolonged my sorrow. By ignoring the full impact of my own actions, I merely accumulated more of what I didn't desire.

At the risk of being misunderstood, life was certainly not all bad. There were many beautiful, fun, wonderful moments. There were times of great joy and excitement. I'm sure of it because I have pictures to prove it. The problem was that I didn't really fully live it. In the aftermath of trauma, my ability to live fully present with great joy, soaking up all that life had to offer was highly compromised. The worst part of that reality is that it escaped my awareness. I had no idea how much more vibrant and rewarding life could be until I dug into the healing work and experienced the difference. In my current practice, it is not uncommon that my clients don't realize how truly unwell they were until they feel better. We are adaptive beings, and oftentimes in our efforts to cope, we neglect to realize just how much we're surviving and not thriving. Even after so much healing, the aftermath of trauma lends itself to fragmented memories, so I am grateful for what was captured in photographs. For anyone who has not shared in the surreal experience of life after trauma, it can be just as difficult to describe as it is to comprehend while you're living it.

After being diagnosed with severe post-traumatic stress disorder (PTSD), high functioning depression, and complex anxiety disorder, I felt a bizarre combination of hopefulness and hopelessness settle in.

The moments when I felt hopeful, my inner rebel was determined to prove the doctors wrong. When my physician had said that some things were unseeable and not to expect to ever be able to function as a normal adult without medication, the gift was in the challenge to overcome those words. It just took me a long while to get there, and that's okay. I loathed the concept of taking medications for the rest of my life, just as much as I hated feeling as though I was half-present. Even on a very low dose, I didn't feel like myself. I resolved that I would utilize it only as long as was necessary. As I began to sleep, I began to heal. I had more good days than bad and, even though the fullness of the side effects of the medications were unavoidable, they became manageable. Until they weren't. Feeling distraught and discontent with a life half-lived, I would discontinue taking the medication. In my worst moments, I struggled severely with impulse control, emotional reactivity, and an onslaught of thinking patterns that included feeling highly suspicious of others, paranoia, and extreme negativity. I had difficulty concentrating, would get easily startled, and found myself avoiding as many people as places as I could for long periods of time, and then rushing back in, to soothe the pain of isolation.

Throughout the years following his suicide, along with shifting between taking medications and not, I also found myself cycling through unhealthy patterns of drinking and connecting with men outside of my integrity. Throughout my years in counseling, I was reassured that it is not uncommon for those who have been abused and endured trauma to seek reassurance, validation, and approval from people who presented similar characteristics to their abusers. Knowing that allowed me to forgive myself and release my shame surrounding my patterns of my past. I would put my daughter to bed at night, have a sitter come over, and go out to the bars and bowling alleys. I wanted some sense of stability and security, and yet my actions were erratic and inconsistent. Though I did my best to protect my daughter from any exposure to or impact of my indiscretions, I felt the weight of failure to be a solid role model for her. I was less present the mornings after a night out, more short tempered, and most likely allowed movies or cartoons to fill in the gaps created by my exhaustion. There is a strong delineation between selfishness and self-care. Sadly, those years were filled with the former, terribly masquerading as the latter.

Around this same season of my life, my sister had invited me to church. I began attending regularly and felt excited to be learning more as an adult about the God that I had been introduced to in my childhood. Though my faith truly did carry me through each season, it was more of a rescue ship that I would send up flare for when I was drowning. I began to learn that instead, the Holy truly desired to be an anchor that kept me from going adrift; an inkling that would take decades to truly come to fruition. It was a very charismatic church that gave me a sense of excitement and connection. Sadly, some of the messages I received were interpreted by my heart and mind in ways that did not align with the truth of Infinite Love I have now come to believe. In the resulting inner conflict, I oscillated further between shameful acting out and white knuckled attempts to uphold the be-good gospel that was far too often preached from pulpits. I continued to struggle with cycles of drinking, taking and discontinuing medications, and seeking the attention and approval of men to soothe the wounds in my heart that I had yet to fully identify. It was as though my draw to the Divine waged war with the unhealed parts of myself, and I repeatedly made desperate attempts to keep each appeased just enough to survive.

In the mix of all those unravelings, I had bonded closely with a man who had been a mutual friend of my late fiancé through grief, as he lost his mother suddenly shortly after my fiancé's suicide. Though we had times of great distance, there was a bizarre pull to him, despite conflicting logic which was silenced. Trauma bonds are among the hardest to break, and at the time, though I had no clue what such a thing even was. I married him in August 2003, an attempt to bring different memories to the difficult season. Mistaking the intensity of such a bond for love, I led myself and my daughter through painful years of connection and eventual abandonment with that man. An entire book could, and will next, be written about that unsustainable mess of a relationship. For now, I'll summarize to say that after suffering a miscarriage, a disconnect settled into our relationship. His out of state job allowed for an easy cover up of multiple affairs, none of which I would learn about until after getting pregnant with my son. We divorced after his refusal to be faithful was made clear, and I became a single mom of two children. My son never had the chance to know his father. Though in differing ways, in my lack of healing, I had continued a pattern of choosing men who abandoned me, and their children.

My faith continued to blossom during that difficult time. I was plugged in at a new church, closely connected with a ministry to mothers of young children. I found great mentoring in a women's Bible study group. It was during that season that I truly began to examine scripture more deeply. No longer was my faith some hand me down version of stories inscribed on me from my youth. I am incredibly grateful for the foundation that had been laid, allowing me to be truly rooted and grounded in love. I also recognize that just as much as a home would be uninhabitable and unable to protect from the storms of life with a foundation only, so was my ground level faith unable to hold me steady amidst the various storms in my own life without the grown up work of growing in my faith. I know it is not easy when we are confronted with life's bad to hold fast to the concept of a good God, and my heart is sensitive towards those who are wading through the hard questions inevitably faced when navigating the tension between free will and sovereignty. For me, freedom was impossible without embracing that paradox. I'll introduce you to more of my process in doing so later on.

I found a rhythm with my kids, my daughter then six years old and my infant son. Between working full time and doing all of the household and child rearing duties on my own, I had entirely neglected any personal fun outside of occasionally enjoying time with my extended family. On the urging of my sister and her husband, I joined them for an Independence Day celebration. While there, I talked more with a man I had known casually for many years. Both of us then divorced, it was suggested that we go to dinner or a movie on occasion. I had no intention of dating, so this seemed like a reasonable solution to still having some kind of social life. We began talking on the phone in the evenings and spending more time together. In doing my best to learn from my past mistakes, I kept my heart highly guarded. I had no intention of seeking any kind of romantic relationship. I had not yet done the healing from the painful abandonment of my son's father. Even so, to be pursued felt good and drew me in. My past patterns of finding security in a man desiring to be with me set the stage for another platform of painful lessons to be learned.

I so desperately wanted a whole family unit. I wanted my kids to have a father figure. I wanted partnership in the joys and struggles of life. He expressed a desire for the same. I had been in counseling, and it was helpful in gaining clarity over what worked and did not work for me. I was clear on what mattered most, or so I thought. In my experience, as well as from what I have come to learn in my personal study of the effects of trauma, what we feel drawn to or comfortable allowing when our nervous system is dysregulated differs significantly from our greatest good, and yet, those compromising choices offer opportunities for growth and personal discovery. Despite significant red flags which my mind seemingly interpreted as bouquets of roses, I married that man in

May 2007. What I would go on to endure throughout that relationship was unspeakable, and deserves to be spoken. There will be more to come in the chapters that follow, as well as in its own book about overcoming the impact of abusive cycles from a relationship where narcissistic tendencies run rampant.

Ultimately, the aftermath of trauma unhealed became an echo of energy drawn back to me in more hurtful and harmful actions and reactions. I was so incredibly unsure of who I was and what I was worth that I promoted more pain through what I allowed. I was haphazardly creating a reality I desperately wanted to be free from. As much as I wish you couldn't relate at all, the likelihood that you can is high. In one way or another, we have all been impacted by ourselves or others who tolerated the intolerable or had moments of struggling to know what to accept, and what to change. Most of us have longed for the serenity that comes from wisdom. Struggle and progress are concurrent themes throughout human history. We are drawn to such stories because in them, we meet more of ourselves.

The overlap of so many life experiences creates a challenge in staying focused on the central theme of this book being the impact, effects, and hope for healing after trauma. I hope that in reading through the messy aftermath you have more grace and compassion for yourself and your loved ones who may have struggled with unhealthy cycles as well. There is a heaviness and hopelessness that bears down when we feel unworthy of what we don't want to allow any longer. There is a harrowing despair that weighs on us when we ignore what we can no longer tolerate, and when we maintain the patterns that make the pain more pervasive. It would take far too long for me to realize that what I was not actively, intentionally changing, I was choosing. I felt powerless to disrupt the devastation that had become my life, just a few months into that marriage. There is a darkness that can settle in when ongoing patterns of having poor aim in life keeps us stuck in cycles of insanity.

Darkness

Deep darkness set in when despite seven years of healing, the fall of 2007, a few short months after getting married, I was once again overcome with emotional unrest, bombarded by an onslaught of unwelcome flashbacks and night terrors as I had been every year prior. The darkness was not due to the ongoing annual realities. No, this darkness was ushered in by unrealistic, unvoiced expectations. Not being my own, those expectations caught me by surprise. What was mine to own was the position I had put myself in, yet again. Not dealing fully with the past traumas led to an unhealthy mindset and further compromising choices for my future, inviting this new wave of darkness into my life through my new marriage. Attempting to move on without the ability to truly move forward inevitably ended up holding me back. Moving on is reasonably easy, in the moment, though it leaves endless traps to fall into later. It is a denial of the impact and aftermath. Moving forward, however, involves a more intentional awareness that comes from mindfully dealing with the events, issues, and resulting outcomes.

Through the years, I had gone from chronically floundering in the fallout year round to a season of several months with the added occasional episode of unrest. That was a victory I celebrated and an outcome that my then husband apparently demeaned as entirely insufficient. Unbeknownst to me, he had presumed that since we were married, my past would be irrelevant. It became his expectation that I no longer suffer the painful problems that had plagued me previously, as though somehow he was significant enough to be my savior. I would have welcomed that reality if it were within my control. No one desires to be overtaken with unwanted grief or undesired memories assaulting their senses. Even so, I was unable to live up to his wishes and thus began cycles of darkness that would go on to feel utterly consuming for years.

In the darkness of my distress, I felt so ashamed of my inability to conquer the dreaded results of my past relationships. With the disturbing patterns of unhealthy communication in my new marriage, I was so caught off guard. I suddenly found myself unsure how to speak, think, feel, or act. I had never felt more unsure or insecure. The way I spoke, dressed, cooked, and cleaned were all subject to his approval that was never granted, though his disdain had not been voiced during our dating. I was thoroughly confused and downcast. The sense of being unworthy of love, care, and kindness from my husband led me down a dark road of codependency. I did everything in my power to coerce myself into becoming who he desired me to be, as inauthentic as it may be. I silenced my sorrows and did my best to dam up my tears. I became an expert at keeping secrets, both of my internal anguish that threatened regularly to consume me, and the external factors of a toxic marriage. Fearing the appearance of failure, I faked a friendliness with my husband, and journaled about sleeping next to the terrorist of my heart. I rationed that I deserved to be treated so poorly for the indiscretions of my past and warranted that somehow I must make this marriage work to protect my children from further loss, regardless of the damage that was created in the process.

There is light in every season of darkness. Though it may dim, I promise you it is there. I have come to believe that the more we focus on it, the brighter it becomes, which is as inherently dangerous as it is beautiful. The difference between the two is a fine line between the good that comes from seeing the silver lining and the bad that happens when we accommodate abuse. There were moments where after dealing disastrous blows to my self-confidence, seeing me in a crumbling mess of emotion, my husband would conjure up gentleness and remorse, and grant consideration for the hardship I was facing. Life would improve for a while; just long enough for me to regain hope in the future. We would create moments of fun and beautiful memories. We would discuss dreams and goals, create action plans to live debt free as he entered the relationship with a far different standard of financial management. We would resolve to train our children up in the Lord, laugh and love to the best of our abilities, and work through our disagreements. Inevitably, I would say or do something that would trip his trigger, and the cycle of demise would begin again. It often felt like two steps forward and ten steps back, and yet somehow in my mind, I reasoned that it was progress. Inherently an eternal optimist, I am quick to give the benefit of the doubt, lending myself to cycles of trust given that had not been gained and were entirely unwarranted.

Far too frequently, my lack of healing found me flailing for any sense of stability I could summon. I would grasp for anything I could hold on to that felt predictable, no matter how hurtful or harmful it may have been. This led to my own poor patterns of relating, communicating in ways that caused my husband to express feeling criticized and controlled. I was quite particular about where things were placed, when things were done, and how routines were followed for our home, especially my kids. My precious oldest who had already endured so much early childhood trauma got the brunt of my motherly dysfunction, as I micromanaged her with an overbearing attitude. When my internal world was crumbling, I wanted to give myself the false sense of security afforded by consistency in my external world, from where the pickles went in the refrigerator to how the food storage containers were organized in the pantry. Though a common characteristic of someone impacted by trauma, my adherence to a more rigid way of life left little room for compromise, and often created a lose-lose dynamic. In the interest of being right, or the false feeling of such, an openness to create a win-win is eliminated. And there is no such thing as a win-lose in relationships.

Admittedly far from perfect, I did pour myself into various resources for learning more about myself and others. Forever fascinated with learning, my childhood pattern of being the classic overachiever welcomed any chance to figure things out. A long time believer that there's always a better way, I would tirelessly examine my routines for efficiency, a great benefit at my job but undoubtedly grueling for my husband and kids. Added to my ongoing fascination with the differences in people, the more I learned, the more I realized how little I knew. I took training opportunities on leadership development, ways to identify and maximize inherent strengths while working to overcome weaknesses, evaluating color personalities as well as other personality profile platforms. Essentially, I was grasping at straws to help me make sense of me, all the while holding on for dear life while the environment of my home continued to rotate from a sense of being absolutely undone to unsteadily rebuilding on an exhaustive repetitive cycle.

In a season of steadiness, while celebrating financial freedom and many positive moments of connection through exciting opportunities to travel, I became pregnant. I learned how to minimize the outward appearances of my internal uneasiness through the fall season when the anniversary of the suicide would come around, attempting to lightheartedly nickname it my "season of suck" (SOS).

He was not generally fond of my nature to shift the heaviness with humor, but it did seem to help even if only slightly. Though he had adopted my older two children, then four and ten, my husband was delighted with the birth of my youngest daughter. Despite a very tumultuous pregnancy wherein my expectations that I would finally have a supported experience proved to be exceedingly unrealistic and altogether unmet, I found myself growing in a new fondness for my husband as he doted on our daughter. Life seemed to improve more substantially than ever before once my mind and body rebalanced from a challenging postpartum recovery, but the darkness lurking around the corner caught me by surprise a year later.

Within this time of darkness, some of the light bursting through was the glorious gift of reconciliation. My late fiancé's family reconnected with me and my daughter. It was a precious promise of hope for the future, and ushered in an invitation for my daughter to be reunited with aspects of her father that I could not fulfill. They were and are truly wonderful people who were also enduring and navigating the messiness of healing from their own grief. True reconciliation is always a prize to be praised. I had to release an unhealthy adherence to the notion that in order to honor my husband, I needed to dishonor the men who came before him. Despite the pain they had caused, I knew this was not healthy for me, or my kids that bore striking similarities in looks and nature to the men that contributed to these precious lives, regardless of how short their tenure. My little loves were the very best of those men, and that deserved to be cherished and celebrated.

Shortly after my youngest daughter's first birthday, we uprooted our family and moved two states south in support of a career opportunity my husband wanted to pursue. This also provided a chance for me to become a stay at home mom. I had grand delusions of what this new life would accomplish for us and hoped for the best. Leaving behind the insurance industry was not a hard decision for me. Leaving family and the stability I had built was incredibly difficult. Though I treasured my role in my home, that fall my SOS rolled in with a vengeance. I had very limited adult interaction and was missing the former co-workers turned friends and close proximity of family that provided a sense of connection and relief. I recall vulnerably telling my husband how hard it was for me and his only response was, "Well, how do you think I feel? Every August, my wife is married to a dead man." I am ashamed to say that his stinging words amplified by the heat and stench of his breath in my face as he towered over me while I sat at the edge of our bed pushed me to a breaking point. I stood up and slapped him across the face. Though I could truly have compassion for the ways my hurt impacted him, I was angered that true to his nature, he simply dismissed me and made everything about him. I was back in a pit of darkness, feeling so cold and low for allowing myself to react so unbecomingly.

The months that followed were increasingly difficult as the goals he had set which moved us away from everything we had known never materialized. We were beginning to feel the financial effects in addition to all the other life stresses. After he changed career paths and the finances improved, we also moved, gaining greater access to a connected support network. The move led to increased connection with a faith community, and once again relying on the Creator to glean insight into the intricacies that made me unique in both gifts and grimaces, grasping for any light to shine on the darkness inside. As I began to feel that warm glow, my more joyful disposition was either met with equal excitement or a forced invitation to join the misery that he seemed content to tolerate. Through all of those changes, I was able to maintain a reasonable sense of balance, free of the medication and accompanying undesired side effects. My SOS remained but was generally shortened to several weeks instead of months. Even in the darkness, there is hope for healing. There is always hope for healing.

It was in that season that I began to grow more in seeing how my attachment of God to those who claimed to love and serve faithfully began to fracture. Closely involved in ministry organizations, I got to see the fallacy of the facade. The smoke and mirrors of organized religion became as evident as the differences between who my husband was in public versus who he was in private. I sought to finally discover in Who and what I believed. I wholeheartedly respect and honor each person's own unique spiritual journey because of my own. I gave myself freedom upon freedom to filter scripture for myself, learning to listen to the spirit within me, beginning to trust my own heart and mind, and finally stop outsourcing my intuition. It was beautifully painful and powerfully challenging. It was in my darkness that the light of Christ in me began to shine more brightly. It was in my darkness that I began to learn more fully that the currency of the Universe is love, not fear.

I will write more in the future about the unspeakable words and actions that ultimately led to my breakthrough, but here, I want to focus on the reality that though the darkness lingered for years, it became easier to see in the dark. I was no longer blinded to the realities of my own shadows, or the downcast nature of those around me. I grew, no matter how slowly, to recognize the ways that certain dispositions would arise in me and how the demeanor of my husband would trigger swift changes in myself. The incurable optimist that was unquestionably curated when I was created was being brought back to life, along with the renegade that refused to accept a life of miserable complacency. That auspicious rebel was delighted to be free of the medication that carried unpleasant outcomes, as the efforts for which I sought it had been achieved. The unseeable was more unseen than not. I was growing in greater resilience and inner stability. The girl in me once fraught with fear was growing in greater self-awareness and gaining ground in regulating herself when the tides changed and the moods of the household were stormy.

Once again, I want to reiterate that there were moments of great joy. The reduction in the intensity of my struggles granted me a greater presence in the moments. We took amazing vacations, played games, ate dinner together regularly, and celebrated many milestones. Were many of those beautiful memories overshadowed by my own dark pain or the immature acting out of my husband? Yes. What matters more is that I was more fully present in the moments. Healing was happening. The books, podcasts, Bible studies, and counseling sessions were slowly, steadily bringing me out of the pit. Each time I fell (or jumped) back in, I got to work to climb out faster and stronger. I am abundantly grateful for the years of challenge that ushered in an ability to self-reflect and fight for my freedom. Especially because, at least in my experience, nearly every great breakthrough is preceded by a breakdown. The light finally more fully breaking through the darkness did not happen for me without tremendous disruption.

Breakdown

"This isn't real" became a mantra for me; a touchstone for my breakthrough, inherently granting me permission to pause and examine the life that played out before me. My son loved reading the Divergent book series, and when the movie was released in 2014, we enjoyed watching it together. "This isn't real," declared Tris as she did a rapid underwater evaluation of circumstances that could have drowned her and instead simply broke a glass tank by merely tapping. In the simulation of her fears, she had the wherewithal to pause and realize it was all a farce. That scene shook me. I felt my mind immediately shift through years of traumatic events and reactions as though I was watching the movie of my life back in triple speed. It was dizzying and delightful. In an instant, I could see it all so clearly. I was deeply disturbed by the reflections my mind allowed me to observe. All of the patterns I had unconsciously promoted, the actions I had allowed, and the mediocrity I had maintained surged through my mind. Although I knew it was all very, very real, at that moment, none of it actually seemed real. And if it was real, I was intent on changing it.

In the first quarter of that same year, I came face to face with the unavoidable reality that my life had become entirely unmanageable. After struggling with my weight for my entire adult life, I had begun healthy eating and exercise routines which caused my husband to make false allegations of infidelity in 2013, the fall and winter prior to the previously mentioned movie release. Disclosing those to a man who was frequently present at the gym was about the very worst decision I could have made. It led to increased communication with him full of inside jokes and inappropriate comments which rapidly turned toxic. Those few months of dishonoring myself and my marriage through unhealthy communication with another man left me feeling utterly shameful. Though short, that season left me in a heap of hurt like I had never felt before. Soon afterwards, I found out that I had been deceived for more than a decade by my husband's own chronic infidelity. The shame of my own indiscretions paved the way for me to promote further passiveness. I crumbled under his criticisms and tolerated the deflections of his shame as he magnified my mistakes and minimized his own. I remember feeling trapped and tortured by my own mind, by the promises unkept, and by the routines replicated.

I once again found myself living as a shell of the woman I thought I was becoming. I stopped my healthy eating and exercise routines, cowered to whatever made my husband comfortable, and catered to his commands in my codependency. Crisis became the only consistency in my home that year. The issues that surfaced in that season triggered the areas of my past trauma that remained unhealed. At the time, this was exceptionally frustrating for me. Now, I have learned that it was truly a gift. We cannot change or heal what we don't acknowledge, so each unfortunate upheaval was a blessing in disguise. I was once again bombarded by mental replays of traumatic events. I felt as though I had taken dozens of steps backward. I was repeatedly told I was crazy, and began to feel it was true. This was also where I would begin to learn that the breakdown was truly a platform for a breakthrough. It took that space of utter desperation for me to accept that these cycles I was complying with were absolutely unacceptable. The ways I was allowing my mind to work were unendurable. The words, attitudes and actions I was using were inexcusable, regardless of the wrongs done towards me.

I am a firm believer that God will orchestrate and align people, places, and problems for our greatest good. Of course that in no way means that all things are good. If there were any way for me to go back and have a similar outcome with less severe circumstances, I would certainly take it. Nevertheless, I would not trade the gains of my growth for a more easy gateway. I have come to understand and even embrace that what I have endured and overcome was all an essential part of my path. Without each moment and milestone, I wouldn't be me. The same is true for each of us, no matter how harsh or hospitable that is to hail. Every hurt, every habit, and every hang up I had along the way were all working together for my good and God's glory. I believe that with every cell of my being. I heard long ago that everything worth the outcome requires effort, and I have experienced this truth in my life far too frequently to discredit or disregard the challenges that change me. God stepped into this newfound season of struggle (SOS) and made meaning out of the mess in ways that would continue unfolding for years.

There is a phenomenal twelve step recovery ministry that became a pivotal platform for my growth and healing in my new SOS. It was challenging for me to step into that space, as I had been hurt by organized religion and truthfully projected my pain inflicted by a husband who proclaimed faith onto other people who proposed the same. Gratefully, I was desperate enough to try it out and found that I was not met with the same hypocrisy and judgment I was determined to avoid. It is a great organization of imperfect people that focuses on the varied hurts, habits, and hang-ups that are common to the human experience, while intentionally connecting with our Higher Power through Jesus Christ. It was an invaluable system of support, encouragement, and accountability. Using the framework and tools of the step study process as well as weekly meetings, I had an opportunity for the first time ever to build a coherent inventory of the events that led to the out of control life I was living, or in my case all too often avoiding. I went on to serve in that ministry for several years and still hold it and the beloved men and women I met along the way in high regard. Though I am no longer connected to this group as a whole, I made forever friends that to this day uphold me in prayer and encouragement, as well as appropriately challenging me when my selections are settling for less than the standards that serve my greatest good.

It also came about that within this SOS, I would embrace the paradox of free will and sovereignty. I would let people be people, and God be God. I severed the threads that imprisoned my perspectives of who Christ was in me from who others spoke of themselves to be, and it was tragically magnificent. Disaster came as I examined ways I had elevated opinions and discounted inner knowings. I deconstructed the projected notions that did not align with truth, and demolished every stronghold that set itself up against the realities of Love in which we are all invited to operate. It happened one tiny moment at a time, and all at once somehow. I was free to choose, and I was powerfully protected by a Conscious Control beyond my feeble attempts. Others were fully free in their own choices, and there was an Omnipotence marvelously orchestrating every detail for the greatest good of all. None of that was anything I needed to readily make sense of; no logic to apply or reasoning to wrap my mind around. My faith became an embrace of power and powerlessness simultaneously that ushered in an unshakable freedom that lingers to this very moment. It is a deep, inner knowing that has a welcome lack of explanation; the essence of faith.

As my breakdown continued to unfold, I became stronger. What I learned about the breakdown is that the only things that truly shatter are those which were meant to be broken. As I sifted through the rubble of a rebellious life and the remnants of wrong turns, I felt a holy invitation to reconstruct only what was authentically me. Before I could usher in this new wave of verity, I had to figure out what that even was; who I was. I granted myself permission to rest, to move, to evaluate, and to explore like never before. I said, "No." A lot. I allowed it to be a complete sentence. I reduced the overwhelming urgency to over explain and simply gave myself the gift of dialing down the ways I had overcommitted and over served. What had become a way of accommodating my shame upended into a way to stop soothing myself through sacrificing who God intended me to be. For perhaps the first time ever, I got very clear on my own thoughts, feelings, and perspectives. I remained curious about the viewpoints of others without actually taking theirs on as my own. Essentially, I was finally truly learning boundaries, and it was painfully beautiful. The people in my life who benefited from my lack thereof were furious and full of accusations ranging from selfishness to questioning my sanity.

I wish I could tell you that my breakdown and the pending breakthrough set me on a trajectory of triumph, but that's just not true. It felt a whole lot more like a hundred tiny breakdowns with the intermittent monumental meltdown, and a feverish attempt to create some kind of masterpiece out of the shards of glass that I used to masquerade under. As I often remind my clients (and myself), healing is a process, not an event. The healing journey routinely resembles something that looks like the random scribbling of a toddler rather than the linear, upward, forward movement that would be desired. Despite a thousand perceived setbacks and missteps, there was an unshakable confidence in my spirit that I would endure; I would persist until I had the success and freedom I desired. I thought back to the words of the doctor nearly two decades prior, "Some things are just unseeable." False. I thought back to the years of struggling to find a medication that never worked without subsequent severe side effects. I refused to return there. I thought back on the seasons of suck and ever present season of struggle, filled with varying degrees of silence and screaming. I thought back on every obstacle that felt like it would overtake me, and I decided to overcome it.

Friend, I don't know about you but I need a momentary reprieve from the weight of it all. I hope you don't mind if I call you friend. It seems fitting since I've disclosed so much of myself to you, though my preference would be if we were sitting across the table, sipping a cup of something warm to soothe our souls as we talk, allowing me to hear your story too. Maybe one day, we'll get that chance. I hope that despite the heaviness and darkness of these past few chapters, you can hang in there with me. We're on the precipice of returning to the light. Just as I disclosed more than once that in the darkness, it wasn't all heavy, I don't want to give you a mistaken notion that the healing journey ends with unicorns. Even so, it is magical. It is freeing, rewarding, and altogether exhilarating.

There are still stressors because we live on planet Earth and it is very people-y here. And if it were for everyone else, no matter where I go, there I am, and the same is true for you. We all come together to individually and collectively offer a majestic complexity to this cosmos. We are all constantly responding to a variety of demands mentally, emotionally, physically and spiritually, both within and beyond our awareness. Life is truly a grand adventure. Despite the ache of abandonment and the terror after trauma, we truly can live lives fully engaged. We have the beautiful opportunity not to become perfect people, but progressing people. We get to reconstruct our lives with meaningful pursuit, joyful expression, and powerful presence. The reality is that if you are reading this, you have a 100% success rate for surviving your very hardest days. Your breakdowns may have been breakthroughs, even if heavily disguised.

That was my story. Breakdown upon breakdown, leading to breakthroughs that I wouldn't bargain for what anyone else may see as a better life. Easier does not equate to exceptional. The most defining breakthrough came for me in June 2019 when my husband told me he wished he could kill me. The dreadfulness of that night caused a significant surge of traumatic responses. My mind was overcome with atrocities I was only able to endure thanks to the years of intentional awareness I had practiced previously. Awareness of intrusive thoughts is essential when the mind becomes a mess. The ability to step back and reaffirm, "This isn't real," becomes a necessity in those moments. I experienced the energy of evil directed at me that night through his words and presence unlike anything I had ever known, of which I will write in greater detail in a book to come. If you have experienced the horrors of relational abuse with a partner who exhibits toxic tendencies like gaslighting, projection, blame shifting, and defensiveness, among other terrible traits, please know that healing is just as possible from that trauma as it is from seeing the unseeable. The events leading up to and following that pivotal point that became a breakthrough were full of traumatic setbacks and a tenacity to change what I could no longer tolerate. I began speaking up firmly against the abuse that had once passively permeated my home.

All the years of my earlier efforts in healing and growth from the trauma of my fiancé's suicide came full circle that fall. Admittedly, I was fearful that the aforementioned traumatic incident would trigger uncontrollable episodes around the anniversary. I experienced understandable waves of anxiety that my previous season of suck or struggle would feel insurmountable. What I experienced instead was the realization that as I held steadfast to my boundaries to no longer allow the unspeakable to influence my life, I was able to stay well. Yes, there were days and even weeks of emotional upset. My sleep cycles were slightly disrupted. Panic was periodically present, creeping up my chest with tightness that felt suffocating. I felt more on edge. My body was still communicating clearly that there was lingering emotional energy that needed to be released. All of these things were minimal in comparison to the years of previous experiences. The responses I continued to wrestle with felt reasonable, and dare I say manageable. And, the unseeable was unseen. My mind was not triggered by flashbacks or night terrors, not of the suicide, nor of the terror months prior. I was free. And you know what, my friend? I have remained free since. I assure you, freedom is worth the fight.

Freedom

Make no mistake, my freedom required a fight. It is highly likely that yours may too. I was called to arms by relationships where others wished me to wager my worth and continue in my codependency. I was invited into battle when my own mind and habits would attempt to convince me to compromise. If, like me, you feel as though you have lost more battles than you've won at times, let me encourage you to get up and keep going. We will lose battles from time to time. If we press on, we will win the war. If we are determined to live in freedom, we won't give up with a small battle lost. We will learn from our losses, and grow in the wisdom, grace, grit, and compassion it takes to continue to conquer.

It cannot be overstated that everything worth the outcome required effort. Being a great mother, grandmother, daughter, sister, and friend has called me to give the best of myself until I know better, and then to do better. Building a successful business and serving my clients with integrity and honor has demanded my utmost presence. Loving others well has called me to higher levels of understanding and celebration of our differences. Down to the simplicity of maintaining my indoor jungle of over 90 houseplants, this too requires effort. My own health in mind, body, and spirit - none of it happens by chance, and neither does personal freedom. Being our best, truly, authentically loving ourselves and others well - this is the war for which we persevere into victory upon victory.

The ability to share openly and freely about my experiences without being overtaken by emotion is still almost unbelievable. It is not just about operating from self-control, and there is no amount of denial or minimization of the severity. It isn't a cold callousness that keeps me calm. Several years now of being free from the onslaught of unwelcome imagery is a beautiful treasure I don't take for granted. And if one day those visions return, I am no less grateful and no less healed. It is not an undercurrent of distrust or disdain that keeps me operating from healthy boundaries. It is an invitation to wholeheartedly value myself and honoring who others show me they are, wisely weighed with their words. I have learned through the years that each sensed setback is only a setup for another level of mending. Nothing changes the prevalence of my past. I was forever changed by the traumas I've endured. I cannot help but trust and believe that I am far more whole through my healing than if I had been given an easy life. I will not arrive at my end unencumbered with unnecessary experience. I will have enlarged my reach and expanded my possibilities with humility and gratitude for the lessons learned. There are parts of my story that will never fully make sense. Even so, I will make meaning of each moment.

There were months when I would shuffle through the heaviness, and then there were weeks. Now, there are minutes, hours, and sometimes days. There are ongoing challenges to creatively explore solutions, and an unequivocal inner knowing that there are far more possibilities for progress than problems that exist. There will always be moments and memories. These are unavoidable actualities of living, and to strip ourselves of these spaces that stretch us would rob us of indelible aspects of our humanity. Freedom, my friend, is not the absence of folly but rather the unshakable assurance that everything is figure-out-able. It is the undisturbed determination to rise up, feel the fullness of our lives, and find passionate purpose in our pursuits. The pursuit of freedom requires the compelling confidence that despite our challenges, and even because of them, we are called to creatively contribute to our communities, large and small, in meaningful ways. In my personal experience, much of that meaningful contribution has come through the greatest areas of struggle in my past.

One of the greatest gifts of my healing journey has been reconnection to myself. I have worked diligently on holding space for myself to learn where in my body I feel the emotional energy associated with various thoughts, recollections, and interactions. This may all sound quite strange; it did to me too. A thought unexamined can do extensive damage, just as much as an engagement with an unhealthy person can wreak havoc on a well-intended relationship. Taking my thoughts captive and truly thinking about what I was thinking about was a learned discipline, just as much as practicing healthy boundaries in my interactions with myself and others. A memory misinterpreted or misrepresented can marginalize or magnify in ways that make forward progress feel impossible. Stepping back when memories would flood me, learning to evaluate them for accuracy, and letting them move through without shutting down or being overcome by them was a slowly built habit. The exercises executed can feel like absolutely awkward practices to entertain initially. With repetition, they become a welcome part of a thriving life of balance. In the next chapter, I will explain more of these routines I implement.

As an avid reader and ardent lifelong learner, I am constantly pouring over books and articles or listening to podcasts and watching videos from a wide spectrum of teachers. A key foundational understanding gained and affirmed from many of these resources was realizing that if the essence of trauma is dissociation, then the essence of healing must be reintegration. Integrating the fragmented pieces, aspects of our lives we would rather wish away - this is essential for our healing. The integration, not avoidance, of our stories is essentially how we begin to live wholeheartedly. For the majority of my life, I had denied my internal warning signs. It is as similarly effective as putting a piece of black tape over your vehicle's check engine light. The breakdown is imminent even if ignored. Closing the gap in the segregation of mind, body, and spirit has become a passionate pursuit, both personally as well as professionally. It requires time and intentional attention to become an observer of our thoughts, feelings, and actions. It takes deliberate diligence to slow down and let ourselves explore each of our senses. It involves serene stillness to silence ourselves and sit with our souls. Taking our brokenness that results from what was done to us and what we've done, letting ourselves release what no longer serves us well, reconcile the pieces, and rebuild in alignment with our authenticity - this is healing.

An aspect of myself that was monumentally damaged from the various traumas I have experienced was my constant questioning of my own intuition. I was severely separated from myself. We are all intuitive in our own ways, and the expedition of learning our own internal language is sacred space. Initially, I had no idea how to differentiate between my internal yes or no. I had catered to criticisms and cowered under coercive control for so long that my internal guidance system was chronically recalibrating. Though my breakdowns and subsequent breakthroughs had led to better boundaries, there was a deeper need in regaining my trust in myself. Essentially, this is the key that unlocks the intuitive network. I can trust myself. I will honor myself. I will uphold my integrity. I will observe and evaluate what is real, not project what I desire. I will listen to myself and others. As a whole, trustworthy person, I will remain connected in my mind, in my body, and in my spirit. I released the baggage of all I had accumulated that was not a healthy part of progress. I no longer needed to carry the thoughts, feelings, and perspectives of others that were inauthentic to me. I reconciled my own unique identity and welcomed the parts of me once denied in an effort to make myself more appealing to others. I rebuilt my life with all the pieces that were truly mine and even gave myself the space to explore what more I wanted in this one big, beautiful life I am given.

Learning to listen to the subtle shifts in my energy has helped me tremendously to learn how to notice and witness my emotions, which are most often highly reactionary and triggered subconsciously. I pay attention when something feels big to me, and when something feels small. Those areas that are just slightly off offer as much growth as those that seem glaringly obvious. Learning to be intentional about my feelings, which are the interpretations of those emotions, has been a fundamental facet of my freedom. In my younger years, I would have not been able to identify, let alone articulate, the difference. It is part of the human condition to have emotions arise in us. I welcome their presence without judgment. It would be, and was for far too long, exceedingly unwise - albeit understandable - to allow my emotions to direct my decisions. As smart and precious as my sweet five-year-old granddaughter is, allowing her to drive my car would be irrational. Likewise was permitting my emotions to run my life. Intentionally bringing conscious awareness, acceptance, and appropriate actions in alignment with the story I attach to my emotions brings balance, accountability, and freedom.

When I want to know more about the attitudes I hold, I look at my feelings - those stories I have attached to my emotions. When I want to know more about my emotions, I look at my thoughts. For me, there has been a direct correlation more often than not, and in these intentional evaluations lies much power for overcoming.

Operating within my personal freedom meant navigating the chasm between not caring what others think of me and caring deeply about how others experience me. The former without the latter would have led me into a spiral of selfishness. If we're not careful, we can trip over that line. The latter without the former could easily have caused me to cave in codependency once more. If we're not careful, others will consume our lives and simply call us caring. I had to fix my busted give-a-damn, learn to filter feedback, and refuse to negotiate my worth with anyone. I had outsourced my value for long enough. My freedom fight was an invitation to get curious about what I truly enjoyed, and let go of what I didn't. Always an adventurer at heart, I gave myself permission to explore in ways that others would likely judge, and do it anyway. I began to fully, ferociously investigate my authenticity. I highly recommend it, whatever "it" is for you. What I have learned is that no matter what we do in our quest for freedom, others will judge our journey. More often than not, in my experience, that is an avoidance of their own. I have learned to filter the feedback I receive, the details and process by which I'll share in another book currently percolating in my spirit. In caring deeply about how others experience me, I give the gift of greater presence and more intentional connection. In not caring about what others think of me, I give the gift of freedom to myself, and them though they may not realize it, to live authentically.

Using the skills, tools, techniques and resources I amassed in an ever evolving and always increasing practice has helped me to hear the whispers of my body. What we do not transform mentally and spiritually we often transfer to be embodied physically. Embracing and loving this body that I used to feel at war with and within has been a priceless gift, even - and perhaps especially - while it remains a work in progress. I have struggled with healthy weight management my entire adult life, the stages set for such within my childhood. Despite that ongoing battle, I am pleased to share that at the age of forty three, I have far less physical pain and disruptive symptoms than I did in my twenties and thirties. I am still doing my work, and always will be. When that work is welcomed with peaceful presence, it becomes an enjoyment, more often than not. Lest the unrealistic expectations arise, just know there are still times of extreme frustration. I spent decades not personally realizing what many of my clients have also learned through my years in practice as a holistic health specialist - what we do not heal we far too often inescapably harbor, and those painful concerns generally fail to be properly addressed. Getting to the root of imbalance and promoting the body's ability to heal itself has been a worthy endeavor for myself and many of my clients. The unresolved emotional energy that lingers physically can create a myriad of manifestations.

Let me tell you what freedom has also looked like: tears, questions, anguish, curiosities, judgments, forgiveness, more questions, and an astronomical amount of acceptance. I have grappled with grief and been entrenched in anger. I have cried countless tears and fought with fantasies until reality became relishable. I have wondered where I went wrong and wrestled with my reasoning until I finally realized the beauty of now was impossible without then. I have told the stories, named the hurts, and granted forgiveness. I have redeemed what was reconcilable and released what remained repugnant. I have wrestled with judgment until I finally learned to fully cultivate compassion towards myself and others. Each of these exchanges unleashed the unnecessary weight of the past and ushered in a light and love that anchors me in peace. I cannot adequately describe the enormity of effort it all required, and even if I could, I would dare not, lest you be deterred from your own undertakings. Had anyone warned me about the challenges ahead, I may have never forged my path to freedom. I'll say again - everything worth the outcome requires effort.

One of my greatest firm foundations of my freedom was solidified by attending an amazing seminar in Texas several years ago. I have gone back and coached that seminar multiple times and have been blessed to watch many phenomenal humans do outstanding work to have big breakthroughs. The energy of the room, the undeniable love and acceptance, and the ability to do the work uninhibited by the outside influences that tend to trip us up made those five days that changed my life forever worth every moment. There were long days of deeply reflective work, and there were moments I wanted to walk out. Choices Seminars went on to be life changing for my younger two kids as well, through their teen camp program. Both programs promoted increased awareness in ourselves, our family dynamics, created important space for safely addressing areas that needed improvement, and gave priceless tools and resources for conquering relational conflict. The relationships forged through that program have made a resounding difference in my life, traveling together and regularly holding one another accountable to reaching our greatest goals. These empowering, healing relationships are priceless treasures. With gratitude for the guidance of each coach, facilitator, and friend I have met through Choices, I am a free and fearless woman, honoring myself and others well by holding space to heal in mind, body, and spirit.

I am somewhere in between who I was and everything I will become. I will always be a work in progress. There is a joyful excitement that most days I almost cannot contain about where this life is taking me. Though I spend several days each year purposely planning and dauntlessly dreaming of the future, the majority of it is largely unknown. Where once before such a notion may ignite fear, now there is a thrill that is indescribable. There is an abundance of gratitude as I reflect back on all I have overcome; years overflowing with beautiful memories and positive learning experiences. There is a freedom from the weight of guilt and shackles of shame that used to keep me chained to the past. There is a freedom to enjoy the day, every day, with a fullness of feeling. There is a commitment to live, not just stay alive, and a contentment with the challenges that granted me the wisdom to know the difference. There is a peaceful serenity in acceptance, and an audacious courage to change.

This odyssey to your sovereignty, independence, and emancipation from all that holds you back may be more strenuous than anything you've ever done. That was true for me, too, so you are not alone. In my personal and professional perspective, it is not entirely uncommon for the recovery to exceed the initial wound in terms of required investment in mind, body, and spirit. A deep cut happens in an instant and takes days to weeks to be made well. What happened to you that creates challenges may have happened in an instant, like my fiancé's suicide. Or it may have been more pervasive and prolonged, like my thirteen year marriage to an emotionally abusive man. Whether your wounds were startling or slowly grew in significance, they are all worthy of the work to be made well. May we all slow down enough to marvel at the miracle of healing and honor the scars that tell the stories of what we've overcome. Make no mistake, my friend, it is work, and it is worth it. You are worth wellness.

Amplifying

I am a big believer that our freedom and healing journey is for us but it is absolutely not merely about us. We break free from all that holds us back piece by painful piece, ideally healing and learning from the challenges we have gone through for the benefit of becoming our best selves. It is for freedom that we are set free, and one of the greatest realities of that freedom is that we each get to decide what freedom means to us. We each have just one life to live, one dash to fill in between the date we are born and the date we retire from our soul's experience in this earth suit. We have but one chance in which we get to choose how we make sense of ourselves and others, how we fulfill our time, and to what and whom we give our energy and attention. We have the beautiful blessing of being owners and creators of our lives. Our lives are not simply the sum of our intentions and ideals, but the collection of the actions and impacts - both those we make and take, as well as those of others that influence us.

It is not merely for ourselves that we fill our time between birth and death. The meaning we make of the middle springs forth from the inscriptions we make on the lives of others. Our healing and growth is also for the benefit of others. The blessings brought to my life by the encouragement of others who have shared their own stories of hope with me have been a beacon in some of my darkest times. I believe this life is truly about how we live, love, and impact this world. Those of us who walk through the darkness amplify our own overcoming by shining a light back for others who are looking ahead for hope that the road somehow, someday, leads to someplace that feels like home, no matter how merciless and strenuous it seems as we walk it. Knowing that someone else has the possibility of traversing their own terrain even slightly more smoothly because I can share insight or encouragement makes my overcoming all the more meaningful.

Throughout my voyage to wholeness, there have been two primary practices that have amplified my efficacy in prevailing, when executed consistently. First and foremost, it was crucial that I rebuild and maintain trust with myself. I did this by repeatedly showing up for myself in new ways to old lessons that kept representing themselves. As I encountered the same predictably problematic patterns with people who were at war with themselves, I simply stopped. I stopped being the collateral damage in their internal battles, often deflected outwardly in destructive ways. I quit trying to reason with those who were unreasonable. I stopped being accessible to those who were withdrawn or evaded accountability at all costs. I quit taking on their projections as any sign of who I am and simply allowed it to be a reflection of how they felt about themselves. I started getting curious about what I truly thought and felt, not reducing my perspectives in consideration of others - just investigating what was authentically me. I started withholding my reasonings and explanations that would be met with accusations of arguing. I started asking more important questions in an effort to understand the real issue, not merely the presenting problem. I started loving myself and others without judgment, and I learned anew what love was and what it was not.

Please don't mistake those simplified stoppings and startings as easy. Honoring my own boundaries and commitments to myself was a strong desire, but the past patterns of pacifying the pernicious people in my path were all too familiar. Every time I responded in a new way to their old games, I reaffirmed my worth. Every time I refused to trip into the traps of their toxicity, I retrained myself to reserve my energy for the battles that mattered the most. It was not selfish to deal with my battles within myself first. That important starting point helped me to ensure I was not projecting and deflecting. From a more healthy internal space, I had the self-control to hold space with and for the stories and struggles of others. I had spent so much time accepting the projected responsibilities of others that I rarely had the capacity to care for myself, let alone maintain the radical responsibility for my own thoughts, feelings, and actions that was required for me to engage in life differently. Essentially, I broke the cycle of reactivity. I started responding, thoughtfully and intentionally. I did not, and never will again, attend every battle to which I am invited. I give myself time and space to consider, thoroughly, the options and perspectives of the circumstances involved in conflict. I grant myself permission to be utterly human. I do the best I can until I know better, then I do better.

The second practice I engaged in proactively was talking openly and often about my experiences, both the successes and the struggles, with safe people. Just as those who teach and tutor solidify their own understandings, so does sharing about our journey help us reinforce our healing. Each time we boldly declare an area of awareness and share the steps we are taking or desire to take, we inherently invite accountability and amplify the likelihood of a more favorable outcome. There is tremendous power in overcoming our struggles through growing in awareness, accepting accountability, and taking appropriate action. All of those are amplified by open communication with healthy people. It is not boastful to proclaim our victories, because true victory hinges on humility. Sharing our success therefore is not a prideful arrogance for power within ourselves, but rather an outpouring of gratitude for the lessons learned and a hopeful encouragement for others who may hear. I have led groups of courageous sojourners, seeking something more than the scraps they settled for. I have been honored to hold the hands of those who have lost loved ones to suicide. I have cried with those who have endured the unimaginable. I have looked dear ones in the eyes and reassured them that even though they may not feel it in the middle of the mess, there is life on the other side of trauma. I have held sacred space for others to feel, heal, and learn to love again - themselves and others.

Safe people can be a difficult concept to wrestle with, especially for those of us with a history of trauma. Our internal guidance system can easily feel like it has a fuse blown or wires crossed. In the beginning of my freedom journey, I didn't even feel safe to or for myself. As I rebuilt my trust in myself and healed in mind, body, and spirit, what I once embraced became intolerable. For me, safety with myself as well as in observing and evaluating the safety of others is essentially about trustworthiness. I became trustworthy for myself. I believed who others displayed themselves to be through their actions and gave their words limited weight. I set a bar for evaluation of trustworthiness in myself and others. I assessed important character attributes of boundaries, accountability, and reliability. I became incredibly selective about who had access to my time and energy. These boundaries of my own were not about seeing myself as more important or better than others, rather, it was about finally fully honoring myself as a valuable woman. I realized what I was worthy of and began to say a hard no to everything and everyone that was not in alignment with words and actions of integrity. No one benefits when we fail to uphold standards of excellence, and we are all worthy of such standards.

Even the unsafe, hurtful, and harmful people are worthy of such standards, for in their implementation, they would likely adhere to greater ways of conduct in life and become far more safe, and far less hurtful or harmful.

I mentioned in the previous chapter that so much of my freedom came through my reconnection to myself and feeling the emotional energy I had associated with various thoughts, recollections, and interactions. Here, I'll expand on those practices and resources I have utilized to facilitate and strengthen the foundations that have helped me build a stable, exciting life. There are several resources available to explore each of these areas further with a simple search. My biggest encouragement is to give yourself the space to experiment with these things and make them your own. For most of these, there is no hard and fast right or wrong way. If I'm being totally transparent, anything that has a firm rule around the way it must be just doesn't resonate with me in general. I'm a challenger by nature. If you are too, you'll likely fully embrace the chance to let yourself feel what resonates with you and make whatever adjustments are necessary. If you are not a natural contender, you may feel more comfortable with stronger guidance. For wherever you find yourself, there are tools and resources to equip you. What resonates with you may change over time and through various seasons. These are by no means all-inclusive or thoroughly explained. These are intended to be ideas, briefly shared to act as an incitement of your own list of habits and practices that enable you to accelerate your healing.

Breathe. Yes, it is as simple (and complicated) as that. Remembering intentionally to breathe and the ability to regulate our breath can feel monumental post-trauma. Slow, deep breathing can stimulate the parasympathetic nervous system, and aid in regulation of the vagus nerve. Through that activation, we are able to become more relaxed, promoting various body systems working together more efficiently, including digestion and heart rate. Intentionally moving your breath in and through your body can also reduce your body's stress response hormones, and have a calming effect on areas of the brain associated with stress and anxiety. I personally practice deep breathing in the mornings and in the evenings, stacking this important habit with several others I'll describe in further detail. I'll finish by giving you an example of my daily practice.

Aromatherapy. The use of aromas has been studied and shown to influence positive emotions, promote relaxation, aid in regulating the mood, and be supportive in trauma recovery. Aromatherapy has a powerful impact on the limbic portion of the brain, which plays an important role in the processing of emotions and memories. The use of Young Living essential oils have been an integral component of my own personal healing journey, and for my family and many clients as well.

Acupressure/Tapping/EFT. Some studies show that applying intentional pressure through tapping on the various energy meridians of the body are effective at relieving stress, anxiety, and negative emotions. As I began incorporating this with my routine, I experienced a noticeable shift. I felt a great amount of release in the emotional energy my body was holding on to in various ways. Restricted and congested emotional energy can contribute to manifestations of pain, tension, and exacerbation of chronic health conditions, and more. Combined with affirmation statements, tapping is an incredibly powerful tool for promoting a sense of balanced well-being.

Counseling. I have been meeting regularly with my counselor for over a decade. We are all constantly responding or reacting to a variety of demands and stressors mentally, emotionally, financially, physically, and spiritually. Having a trusted professional who has experienced me through the many stages of life, can remind me of the growth I've accomplished, reflect back important questions for my consideration, and help me keep my mindset right is a priceless resource. I may have started counseling because I felt exceptionally broken. I continue because mental health maintenance is a substantial aspect of me staying whole.

Connection. Trauma and the associated reactions can feel and become quite isolating. Building a trustworthy community around myself has been pivotal. Connection brings a sense of joy and vibrancy to life. It allows me to hear and care deeply about the experiences and perspectives of others, and to have that same consideration reciprocated. These valuable relationships also provide much needed accountability. Through these trusted friends and family members, I am appropriately challenged, encouraged, and empowered to continue to be my best self. I understand that at times, the community we're immersed in can be a key contribution to our stressors, making this important aspect of connection more challenging. Whether that is true for you or not, you may benefit from thinking outside the box about connection points. Some of my greatest breakthroughs and points of connection have come through attending various seminars, retreats, and other healing events. I believe our needs for those resources elevate when our more immediate circles are part of what keeps us spiraling in cycles of struggle.

Grounding. There is no substitute for being connected to the earth. Studies have shown that taking time to ground ourselves, as simple as standing in the grass - or my favorite at the beach - barefoot, may balance cortisol levels, improve sleep quality, reduce inflammation, and bolster immune function. Getting outside barefoot daily is ideal. Building in this habit as often as possible is a free, easy way to support a balanced sense of well-being.

Sunshine. I have jokingly assessed that I am basically a houseplant with complicated emotions. Give me the right soil (environment), sunshine, and water, and I'm happy. Sometimes, it truly is that simple. Sunshine aids in our synthesis of Vitamin D, can support a healthy circadian rhythm, and has even been shown to promote balanced blood pressure, among many other benefits.

Faith. By now, I hope it is entirely clear that the ability to overwhelmingly conquer is mine, and yours too. My tattoo on my right forearm reminds me over and over again of this beautiful truth from Romans 8:37. Whether we share the same perspectives of faith and religion or not, we do share the reality that we are created with purpose and greatness. You're living proof that Divine Love exists; your breath in this very second evidence that you were intended to be here. I believe faith, in whatever way you define and decide to allow it to indwell in your life, is a crucial component to thriving. I cannot imagine where my life or the lives of my children would be without our faith anchoring us through the storms of life.

Foundations of Wellness. This is easily one of my favorite topics to teach on, when the opportunities arise. Getting excellent sleep - ideally 7 to 8 hours for adults, taking in excellent nutrition through consuming real food - not the processed, packaged junk, and drinking adequate pure, clean water are all essential elements of a healing journey. Many of us are educated far beyond our level of obedience, further proof that healing is a progressive practice, not a one-time event. Give yourself grace enough to avoid shame, and effort enough to make a change. Movement through healthy exercise and engagement in activity is another critical constituent of health in mind, body, and spirit. If these areas are a struggle for you, take them seriously. Seek professional advice and more ardent accountability where necessary. Slow, steady changes are often ideal in building a foundation of wellness. I found that when I attempted to change too much too fast, I was far more likely to oscillate between extremes.

There are so many other tips and tricks I could share from music to movies, podcasts and books to fun activities, seminars, and on and on. What it truly all comes back to is that there are infinite possibilities and unlimited potential as we pursue our growth. It would be as easy to get overwhelmed with the area of personal development as it is to freak out once you start examining chemical toxicity in the average household. You may end up wanting to overhaul everything instantly. Too much too fast is an easy way to feel burnout. Find a small starting point, and then expand gradually as you gain traction. I advocate for stacking up habits as much as possible.

For me, this looks as simple as taking a few deep breaths when I wake up in the morning as I am tapping on a few of my favorite energy meridian points while also intentionally speaking affirmations for my day. I grab for my essential oils and apply whatever I intuitively reach for, trusting it to be what I need to bring a balanced energy and excitement to the day. In the evenings, I am starting my essential oil diffuser for aromatherapy while I sleep and back to those same deep breathing techniques with tapping and reciting statements of release, letting go of the stresses of the day. Additionally, I have my bi-weekly counseling sessions and attend a weekly Bible study group, as well as worship services on many Sundays. Maximizing my healthy habits throughout the days, weeks, and months, you may see me grabbing a book to read outside while I soak up sunshine and get connected to the earth, or listening to empowering podcasts while I workout. I am intentional, though entirely imperfect, in my meal planning as well as scheduling times to connect with others. None of these patterns were instantaneous. All of them require effort and personal accountability.

I am blessed beyond measure that the work I do rarely feels like work. I naturally get to reinforce my own healing while holding space for amazing men and women to heal in mind, body, and spirit. As a holistic health practitioner, I am actively involved in coaching my clients and supporting their great goals and growth. And now, I am abundantly grateful to get to expand my reach to you, dear friend. This work has been decades in the making, and required another level of overcoming to bring it to print. Thank you for the privilege of trusting me enough to read my reflections. Life can feel as exhilarating as it can feel challenging. It truly is a grand adventure. I hope you live it fully. I hope you overwhelmingly conquer every challenge that dares a threat to hold you back. I hope you believe in the miraculous healing that is your right, and fully embody the righteous responsibility to pursue the greatness and purpose for which you were divinely destined. Until next time…

Kristin

About the Author

Kristin Campbell, N.D., is a certified holistic health professional, passionate about empowering others to live well in mind, body, and spirit. Refined in the flames of her own personal healing journey, she seeks to inspire all she meets to promote their own wholeness and freedom. Through the active, ongoing pursuit of a purpose-filled life, compassionate care of her clients, and dedication to life-long learning, she embraces opportunities to combine intellect and intuition with authenticity and love.

Kristin is a mother of three amazing kids, bonus mom to many more, and grandmother to one precious girl, and hopefully several other grandchildren in the future. She is abundantly blessed in lovingly connected relationships with friends and family, near and far. Whether with family, friends, or on adventures alone, she enjoys travel and the fearless immersion of living a vibrant life, full of experience.

As an author, speaker, and life coach, from her wellness practice to hosting retreats, Kristin welcomes chances to positively impact the lives of others. With a warm-hearted, vulnerable approach, she brings insightful energy to a life of meaningful service, seeking to leave each space she enters better than she found it, encouraging others to do the same. Believing we are all created with greatness, purpose, and unlimited potential, she unfailingly encourages the best in herself and others.